LYRIKEDITION 2000

founded by Heinz Ludwig Arnold[†]

published by Florian Voß

Allitera Verlag

LUDWIG STEINHERR was born in Munich (Germany) in 1962. He studied philosophy and earned a PhD after submitting a dissertation on Hegel and Quine. He lives in Munich. For the twelve books of poetry that have been published so far, he has received various awards, such as the prestigious *Leonce-und-Lena-Förderpreis*, the Book Award of the Evangelical Churches in Germany, and the *Hermann-Hesse-Förderpreis*. Since 2003, Steinherr is a member of the Bavarian Academy of Fine Arts. His work has been translated into multiple languages. He has been invited to various internationally acclaimed literary festivals, such as the *Journées Littéraires de Mondorf* (Luxembourg), *German-Arabian Poetry Salon* in Damascus (Syria), as well as the *European Literature Night* in London, *StAnza - Scotland's International Poetry Festival*, and the *Birmingham Literature Festival*. In 2012, he was lecturer at the University of Notre Dame (USA) in the *Advanced Lecture Series*.

Recent publications include »Das Mädchen Der Maler Ich. Collected Poems« (2012), »Ganz Ohr« (Lyrikedition 2000, 2012) and »Flüstergalerie« (2013). Along with »All Ears«, »Before the Invention of Paradise« (Arc Publications, 2010) is also available in English translation.

PAUL-HENRI CAMPBELL was born in Boston (MA) in 1982. He is a bilingual poet and translator and lives in Cologne, Germany. Campbell is the co-editor of the annual anthology »DAS GEDICHT chapbook. German Poetry Now.« Recent publications include: »Space Race. Poems|Gedichte« (2012) as well as »Am Ende der Zeilen | At the End of Days« (2013).

Ludwig Steinherr

All Ears

Poetry

Translated and supplemented with an essay
by Paul-Henri Campbell

LYRIK
EDITION
2000

Visit the publisher's website in order to find additional information and other great books:
www.allitera.de

Further information on the Lyrikedition 2000 is available at
www.lyrikedition-2000.de

November 2013
Allitera Verlag
A publisher in the Buch&media GmbH, Munich (Germany)
© 2013 Buch&media GmbH, Munich (Germany)
Layout: Carolin Pollak, Munich
Copyediting: Sarah Cossaboon
ISBN 978-3-86906-608-0

The Secret Dominion

Geheime Welt

.

The Secret Dominion

Turn off the light
and cloaked in darkness a mad party begins –

Wonder what they're up to in the dark
sofa coffee table pictures shelves
every which way –

mystic drinking sprees
metaphysical orgies of which you
haven't got the faintest idea –

Only if you drowsily stagger
into the living room
touching the light switch –

The startled look of the floor lamp
as though it just had been
traversing sun moon and stars making out
with an archangel

Garden in the Night
When Nobody is Watching

The hour at which every bush
begins to be fragrant with the odor of
a lady's shawl left behind on the terrace

The hour at which the ants are searching for a signal
from the star that radio controls them

The hour at which the heartbeat in the trees pauses
-----
until some cat's sudden shriek reanimates it

The hour at which Love's spell showers down
from every bough and twig and drives them crazy
only them: the grass and the bugs

The hour at which the first newspapers are delivered
still damp from the black blood – and every letter
an Apocalyptic Horseman

The hour at which Anubis God of the Dead
forces his jackal head through the fence
and wanders through his territory

While Brewing Strong Coffee

This afternoon is a fly
locked up in Caravaggio's cranium –

I hear it buzzing
a gorgeous impetuous blow-fly
one only the Baroque period could birth:
glistening with every shade and hue of sin

It nips at the painted wine goblet
sucks on the pallid nipple
of the juvenile Bacchus – in vain

It crawls over the callow skull of Abraham
and is now scuttling across Judith's décolleté
as though it were following the scent of blood
from one assassination scene to another –

But it is already in flight again
entering deeper into the dark labyrinth of the atelier
losing its bearings amongst the stretched canvases:
hurried drafts
glowing scenes that haven't been created yet
paintings that Caravaggio will never paint
but still exist –

just like the fly that nobody sees
with only its deep hum audible
as it teeters on
from light to darkness
from darkness to light
intoxicated
by the bewitching scent
of fresh crimson paint
as though taken from the slaughterhouse

In the Darkness Your Third Shoulder Blade

Im Dunkeln dein drittes Schulterblatt

Arrival, Too Early

Just a moment!
says the Babylonian slave girl at the reception
Your room will be ready shortly!

And the linens still warm with the love
of Héloïse and Abélard are swiftly changed

Agamemnon's blood is drained from the bathtub –

Hans Castorp's cigar butt disappears in the trashcan –

The paper napkins
heavy with the phlegm of The Lady of Camellias
and Verdi's crumpled up sheet music
are tossed into the same plastic bag –

A hand adjusts the *Lapis Niger*
as a paperweight –

The pillow
that suffocated Emperor Tiberius

is decorated with a chocolate heart –

and prettily placed
by the winking maid
Cassandra

In the Museum and Afterwards In the Rain

I

Juicy melon slices
viewed close up are suffused
by cobwebs of fissures
and the faces of women in golden frames:
they all act
as though death wasn't their business –

We are bathing our eyes
in their glamour
turned away from us –

But the dance floor groans
at every step
like an invalid
pained by the softest touch

II

As we step into open
I fondle your warm nape –

That moment falls down
like a mercury thermometer

falls in slow motion
and shatters –

the silver pellets
roll about everywhere

impossible
to catch them again

with bare hands

so lustrous
so viperously fast

they reel about and
split up infinitely

roll into
cracks and crannies

gone forever

for Katrin Sonnenschein and Hannes Fricke
on October 15th, 2010

Hallowed Twilight

Since when does your silence have
this gentle S-motion of a Gothic Madonna
who misses her child?

Since when have your shoulders
and loins and breasts
been sprouting
curl after curl
soft and fluffy hair
like in the miracle beckoned by St. Agnes?

The fragrance of linden wood emanates from your skin
invisible angels are carrying you upwards
high above my ash-grey hairline –

I want to call upon you
but I stand here immured
by this semi-darkness –

creatures
all sorts of strange ones
and tendrils and leaves
are growing forth
from my mouth of stone

Side Chapel

You mute martyrs
shackled fettered muzzled by your
gory legends –

you skinned roasted disemboweled creatures –

have a chat with me!

Saint Agatha of Sicily –

for a moment, forget
your severed breasts
that you carry around
on a platter like two tortes

and tell me about your childhood
about the scent of thyme in the shadows
and about your first seashell necklace –

Just once let your
shawl waft from your tomb
not because a volcano is erupting

just because –

out of joy

Naked

In the dark I have
found and touched
your third shoulder blade –

I've discovered the birthmark
deep down in your soft palate
the sanguine host –

I know now: your little knuckle
is a Venetian poison ring
I slurped up every last drop of it
however without dying –

I have heard the rustling of your soul
as it rose above the sleeping corpse
at daybreak
and stepped into the open door
shivering –

Naked you stand before me

and whisper your innermost
secret to me –

I always knew it:

You're invisible!

Roman Nocturnal Stroll

This darkness
so soft so draining:
an assault –

Floral scent from behind my back
presses a razor to my throat –

This is how easy one could meet death!

The guy over there spray-painting
phallus symbols on the walls of a closed tavern
is Catullus –

He wants to die!

Because Lesbia is sitting inside
cooing amongst her numerous lovers
and is amusing herself behind closed shutters –

Sometimes you can hear her giggling, softly!

Or is it simply madness –
is she already beyond the horizon
lustfully undulating in someone else's bed –

and in the dark
only the tables
and the stacked chairs
creakingly carrying out
their metaphysical
nighttime dialogue?

Looking at Your Photo on the Plane

With every mile between us
your complexion grows more ethereal
you vanish deeper
into the light of a 19th-century atelier –

What an apotheosis!

You remove yourself
you are removed up to them
those solemnly-pale goddesses of the daguerreotypes
who fade away in the invisible gallery
during this nightfall in January –

Women with such far-flung eyes
as though they believed in mesmerism
lavender pillows and Plato's ideas –

They are sitting uprightly for they are bearing candles
snow falls upon their parted hair –

They all have the same nightmare:
to be the only one naked
amidst the excitement of a ball –
any moment someone could notice!

Instead they are behind glass tightly laced into their corsets
they can hardly draw a breath

But a dreaming look
at their dreamt nudity
sends a tremor into the candles held by their fingers
and sets their countless skirts ablaze

Motionless they are sitting
within the flames
and are unable to make a stir –

Motionless you are now sitting here
furiously flaming in front of my eyes
in a dark frame

mutely staring at passage of the icy winter clouds
those armies of the 19th century sweeping by

while you burn up like a comet
in front of my eyes in divine nudity
upon an airplane sky

Forensics

We've hardly emptied our cups
as the forensic team enters the room –

Every glance every gesture
a moment ago still freely hovering in the room
is now collected labeled
lipstick fixed on vowels
Forceps picking every consonantal chip
out of a napkin
Blood particles on an aspirate
held under a lamp
appear in a blue fluorescing mysticism
Even the hidden dreams
leave their fingerprints
which the dusty brush gingerly
brings to light –

Ah, only a fool could believe
a lost eyelash would remain undiscovered
a *Spiritus asper* would be without consequences
in the face of fanatic judicial administration
within this cosmos!

The Museum of Beautiful Ideas

Museum der schönen Ideen

Shop Window with Antiquated Leica Cameras

You archaic devices of hell
lurking there maleficently –

Until your only crocodile eye
snaps
and consumes the next best moment –

You gobble it down into the underworld
headfirst in the terribly awry Orcus
into the inverted world
of negative images –

And there we sit at the table
the funeral banquet
black faces
grinning luridly
surrounded by blazing white hair
beneath a black ashen sky –

Only the blackest magic can save us
occult rites
amidst red shimmering light –

so that we ultimately do
resurface as gleeful companions
from the developing tray –

euphorically soaked and dripping

reclaimed from the Hades

The Museum of Beautiful Ideas

I merely set foot into it for a few seconds –

to catch a glimpse
of this stray hair in Aphrodite's armpit
that curls and twirls like an elated zeta

or of the little toenail
of baby Jesus
in a medieval miniature –

Then I flee quickly into the atrium
(always peaceful and cool)
and sneak in
a strictly prohibited cigar

until the smoke
rushes tears into my eyes

Blizzard in the Night

Teeming particles in the beams of the headlights
Billions of swarming sperms
competing hotly for a single egg cell
that does not exist –

They all tumble into emptiness
hurled into the cosmos by one
logos made sleepless by its tenderness –

They will not fertilize anything
They will be lapped up
by the endlessly dark road –

Others however lay there
nearly untouched
white cold pure
like the tiles in a Lady Chapel

persevere throughout
the eternity of a nocturnal voyage

until the first light
intones the lauds

Black Painter

You
who is laying restlessly in his bed
as upon the planks of swaying scaffolding
suspended over the abyss of a grim cathedral –

You
who is plunging into the ashes of Troy
the brush made of Cassandra's eyelashes
and bedewed with a drop of blood
from Christ at the Column –

You
who is painting his black frescos
upon the sweat-soaked brow of the ceiling
apocalyptical scenes
invasions collapsing stock markets volcanic eruptions
jingling processions
into the abyss –

You least favorite of gods and mortals!

No child leaves the ball out on the street
and stares over your shoulder with bated breath –

No chickadee flutters by
in order to peck at your noxious fruits –

Only the eagle that torments Prometheus
visits you regularly
and takes a rest perched on your breast

and its beak is
black black black

and sharp

pointed like your brush

White Painter

You need no canvas
no colors!
Your eyelashes will do
for brushes!
Each of your works emerges
from a single blink of an eye –
Favorite of the Gods!
On your strolls you wander through
the endless workshops of this morning
and pass through white walls –
nothing can stop you!
A Pope of the *quattrocento* would hold the mirror
up to you for a self-portrait!
In the whitest bed your naked courtesan expects you:
the light!
You have spawned countless bastards with her
who unfortunately all
turned out to be painting in black

In the Bamberg Cathedral

The girl of stone
with the tender locks
and the dress sticking to her skin
(as though she had come in from a sudden cloudburst)
she is *Synagoga* –

She has been blindfolded
for she is supposed to be blind to Truth –

This ought to turn into a poem
about pogroms and smoldering ovens –

But I am only able
to think about the musty varieté show
in which she the psychic could foretell
whatever this summer morning assisting her
is about to pull out
of my pockets with his glowing fingers –

a return ticket to Munich
a mechanical pencil made by *Caran d´Ache*
7 Euro 38 in small change
and an unfinished love poem

that she is reading to me
in *sotto voce* syllable by syllable
as though it were
composed for her

Giorgio de Chirico

The house is without roof
There are no stars

The light – a wafer-thin layer
of pollen
dusting the furniture
of this forlorn afternoon –

Or has the night come yet
without our knowledge?

On the floor above us
the marbled goddess rocks blindly
upon her base –

armless she scrabbles her way
through the clutter and muddle
of the nocturnal cosmos
of the slanting Orcus
blind like the creatures residing
at the depths of the sea
she bumps into everything
grabs shards of glass razorblades
with her non-existent fingers
She trips and falls terribly –

We hear her fall
and are unable to aid her –

We ourselves are sitting in the dark
even though it is light –

We are forbidden to move
to take a breath!

The pollen vague like a childhood scent –
One breath and it would be gone –

The candle of the spirit has been blown out –

The night now is rising
down onto our floor –

We have already gone blind –
Gods
without arms in the darkness

The Sensuous the Utmost Abstraction
(Hegel)

We fanatics of abstraction!
How abstract is this glass of wine
with the traces of lipstick upon it!
How abstract is the sip of Merlot upon the palate!
How abstract is the chicken leg you're gnawing on!
How abstract is the first drop of rain that touches
your forehead now
and the one that is running down your breast
after having fallen into your blouse!
How infinitely abstract is
our insatiable cannibalism
that compels us to sink our teeth into one another
how vexingly vexingly abstract
this momentous flare of a match
sparked by the breathing body –

And yet we are once again
under the most concrete showerhead
standing in the roaring spray of the
waterfall of the absolute
that could soothe our thirst
eternally –

if I the incurable fetishist of the abstract
would not once again
desire to lick
this one little
abstract droplet
from your supremely abstract shoulder!

The Sculptor Says

I've studied the anatomy of shadows –

Innumerable Gods have been lying on my dissection table –

Did you know
that each one of us possesses an organ
with which we receive the silence of stones?

Somewhere between the collarbone
and the third eye it constantly migrates –

Its shape is reminiscent
of a lost silk shawl
on the autumnal pathway
somewhat uncertain of its existence

Its color – hard to say!
It fluctuates between invisible and purple –

Just like that – yes, just like the shawl
that presently slips from the armrest
of your silence
and wafts away
weightlessly
through Orcus and light

for Josef Alexander Henselmann

The Ghost Train with Living Ghosts

Geisterbahn mit lebenden Gespenstern

The Sudden Jolt of Autumn

What madness!
The maple tree right
in front of our very window
has drenched itself
with gasoline
and set itself on fire!

No idea
what it's protesting against!

Just ignore it!

Localization

We live at the periphery
in the green shaded suburb of suffering
where squirrels sit upon the mailboxes
and only sleeping pills
stare sleeplessly into the emptiness –

From here the trembling finger
slides across the stained city map
across factories
smoking landfills
oncology wards
slaughterhouses slums
and military installations

toward the center

that is always
in flames

where black
bodies voicelessly
bend
like wasps
on the stovetop

Finale

Now
the black coffer
closed over you –

Now
the great illusionist mounts the stage

He draws
sword after sword
out of the pierced heart
of the sorrowful Madonna
in the Side Chapel

and plunges it into the coffer
blade after blade –

The bored trees behind the staging
the gleefully murmuring rain
they know:
it's only a trick!
I will see you again!
You will emerge from the coffer
unharmed at the end of the show
return to me smiling –

But the coffer is black –

I am barely able to stare at the swords –

the sanguine handgrips
the glistening tips

Library in Evening Light 1

O weary capital of Gods!
O dusty pyramids!
Offerings! You demand offerings!
Else your world will expire –

I am sitting alone under the withered
feebly glowing sun
the fifth sun with the farrowed face
that is sticking out
its tongue further and further
thirsting
for human blood

Armageddon

In slow motion the comet plummets
down silently –

It is very bright and smells of fire –

Hysteria everywhere and scrimmage:
Delete the files! Destroy the archives!
Spray blood with fire hoses
from cellar cells!

I crumble up my page
and stuff it into my mouth –

Everybody knows what was on it –

But I gulp and gulp

Eye in eye
with the comet

that is falling so slowly

as though it stood still
in the sky

Cassiopeia Rests Her Finger on Her Lips

Have you seen the alley lined with poplars
standing there so solemnly hushed?

She is listening

At the hour of the execution
the guards draw near clandestinely on felt slippers

Nobody knows the moment
but everybody is aware of the rumor

As long as steps are audible clanking about the cobble stones
there is no danger

But now it has been silent quite some time

The poplars are listening

Make noise!

No dreams cost what it may!
No felt slippers!

The Ghost Train with Living Ghosts

Even on this milky autumn morning
the voyage continues on –

The light scarcely sees through fingered shadows –

I try to imagine the trees
without masks and beards –

Faces that slither towards me
are disfigured from the cold –

Viewed from the outside the universe
is tiny and inconspicuous like a lost glove

and yet we have gone astray
lost in his bent fingers
as though the darkness were endless –

Those who find a way out
are grey from terror
or had their eyes shut
the whole time

Gunfight at the OK Corral

1881 –
faraway in Paris the ten-year-old Proust is musing
about the taste of a Madeleine in the lime blossom tea
and is assailed by his first asthma attack
during a stroll with his parents in Bois de Boulogne –

And then Wyatt Earp, Doc Holliday
and the rest of them
load their Colts
chamber after chamber
with eschatologically blinking
.45 bullets
and walk down the endless road
in dusty boots

under the same heaven
so metaphysically pervading light
as the heaven of the Last Judgment
in the *Sistina* –

30 seconds – 30 shots

Three men in the sand
covered in blood
with the ferocity of archaic lightning bolts of the gods
expelled from this reality
into another –

Each one of them
infinitely removed
amongst their bare teeth
the aftertaste of some sort of taste
infinitely stranger
than the one of a Madeleine
in lime blossom tea –

Le temps perdu –
Le temps retrouvé –

While the pragmatists of metaphysics
under the apocalyptic heaven of the Sistina
in which Proust just happens to be studying
the Sephora's drowsy gaze with his lorgnette
empty out their bullet casings
into the blood-drenched sand
and are reloading their Colts
chamber for chamber
with gleaming lightning bolts

Library in Evening Light 2

A moment ago the master was speaking to me –

whispered a word in passing
that nearly blinded me
with its lightness –

Now the master has died –
dissolved in a mass
of rotting flesh –

How could he do that?

He might as well
could have put a paper helmet
upon his head and crawl about
yowling on all fours –

and I am sitting here
trying to remember that word –

fingers in my ears

in order not to hear the beastly clamor
of the master

Dark Autumn Afternoon –
A demon whispers to me
or is that my own voice?

The world within and the world without
indistinguishable –

The soul is spread out on the table
like an inverted glove –

A bitch feigning pregnancy
is haunting the house
wandering about searching
for its imaginary boy
and is licking the milk
from her teats and whimpers

Maybe Gold

This November afternoon is watching me
as I pour the tealeaves into a tin
is watching me with the large
dark eyes of a little girl

I don't know – is she mute
or is she refusing to talk?

Her hands are hidden behind her back
as if she had stolen something
or was bearing a knife –

Maybe she has no hands?

Maybe she is shy
and could spin straw to gold?

But she remains silent
and is peeping over my shoulder without a stir
in the twilight

where the maples are gesticulating
their tops like madmen

Rain in the Night

Black blotography
picture for picture –

Is this going to be a Rorschach test?

I try to recognize something –

The gondola glides forth without its helmsmen
the two *Gondolieri* have dozed off
in their winter coats –

The star perceives itself in the mirror
as a demon –

All organs of silence
are arranged in pairs
like stamens in a priming flower –

Isn't that a miraculous coincidence?

But the invisible analyst
doesn't say a word –

Perhaps he's sleeping
behind his inanely flitting lenses
perhaps he has long
left the cosmos –

Only his enormous
black fountain pen
is on the table
with its blazing golden nib
and is dripping
and dripping

A Melody in Every Entity

Too many voices are in the air
a confused jumble of talk –

Even the unconscious stones are stirring
twitching with the eyelids

Has God under-dosed
their anesthesia today?

Their murmurs
too horrifying too obscene
to not be the truth –

Heraclites covers his ears
but he understands each syllable

Night in November

Who shattered the street lantern?

Are there no stars here?

Once seafarers navigated
across the sky
because the world was so gloomy
and the drooling ocean
wild and full of gruesome behemoths –

The same frothy chaos is up there now –

Maybe the seafarers drowned?
Maybe they have long since arrived?

Occasionally
they send postcards –

Strangely though:
they all seem to have been
written by my hand!

Untouchable

A winter's evening – dark as the one
when I carried my doll to the doll's doctor –

Oh, she's naked in the cold!
a girl's voice cried

When I pushed the door open
a bell clang
as though I had shattered the China
in the palace of the pixies –

The doll's doctor with an artificial leg
with a glass eye
bowed down from his stately throne
grunting at me –

Half of him belonged to the pantheon
that was lined up in the shelves
each figure with a vacant stare –

With one quick motion
he tore off the dandling limb
and held the little arm up like a cannibal
then he dragged the doll into his cave –

I remember
something floating
from her white torso –

something that looked
like the dirty snowflakes
now outside the window
so forlorn so helpless

and that I didn't
dare touch

ORANGES MOVING IN

ORANGEN IM ANROLLEN

Oranges Moving In

1
Here comes the sun!

2
Beg your pardon! But we simply are
the sunny boys in the Lord's creation!

And shouldn't you be aware of it:
in German, »Optimismus« is spelled
with a capital »O«

3
Dammit if we were to be
ashamed of our
perfect bodies!

4
And don't you forget:
we cast a conservative vote!

The only God there is
is tubby and orange –

and secretly dabs himself
with our paradisiacal
Eau de Toilette!

5
We are really sorry for you
you flapping marionettes
with your twisted arms and legs –

your invisible strings are forever tangled up
in that Gordian knot
you call *Geist!*

No wonder
that you're haunted by nightmares
and only sever your own strings
with Ockham's razor!

6
You even turn sex into
an exam on Euclidean
and Non-Euclidean geometry –

All those angles axes of symmetry parabolae!

Wavering sine and co-sine curves –

Believe us!

Everything you may be lusting after
is a fully inflated
radiant ball!

We are those perfect spherical beings
that Aristophanes babbled about!

We know what self-love means!

By the way:
»Orgasm« is capitalized, too,
with an enormously large »O«!

7
Don't act so aloof!

If you sting us – we do not bleed?

But even our blood
is as yellow as the sun –
and a vitamin boost along with that!

Throw us on the back of a truck
Pack us in a cattle wagon
force us in boxes and nets
quarter us divide us in eighths
mince and dice us
squeeze us out in the juice extractor –

We are radiant!

Radiant
until the archangels cry and applaud!

8
Seriously now:
in the cosmic finale
human mass: orange mass –

Who does the light cheer on?

9
To be or not to be –
not a problem for us!

Hand over an orange
to Hamlet instead of his skull!

Death?
Okay! We're ready!
Let's go!

For us it is simply a massive push –

and there we roll
across God's eternal golf course

Spiral Staircase of Snow

Schneewendeltreppe

Afternoon Show

You came
mysteriously
like the magician's assistant

the finger on your lips

you spread out on the bed
so lost in thoughts
so removed

so that your body
began to hover –

An invisible hand
drew a golden ring around you –

and in the next second
you were gone –

Now I am wandering
aimlessly in the dawning coulisse of this evening
and I am searching for you
amongst mirrored doors

while out of
all my pockets buttonholes sleeves
the most bewitching
flowers of wonder
are sprouting forth

House of the Spirit

Dear Ludwig Wittgenstein
you envisioned a tree house
as the VIP lounge for the immortal gods
strung up upon a thread of nothingness –

without a tree, of course
and the ladder toppled over –

But the haunted and restless spirit
dwells in ruins –

Lightning bolts shatter the windowpanes
weeds grow in the cracks of the pavement and sprawl –

Yes, the house of the spirit
is always *a haunted house* –

Martens are squirming and rattling in the attic
hornets' nests are buzzing –

There is the thundering
of bowling balls or rolling skulls
and the ocean's surf
that doesn't exist at all –

In the twilight of the evening chamber
Orestes is sitting calmly without a stir
petrified
while the clock is ticking
the bloody blade on his lap
and is waiting for the Erinyes –

And if I am lucky
the *White Lady*
will visit me in moonlit nights –

Never do I know
if she is a wave or a corpuscle
or an amorous dream –

Never do I see her wholly
only from the corner of my eye
as her heel
her glove
her rustling skirt hem

vanishes
around the next corner

Chapeau Claque

This winter's night
pulls us magically out of the *Chapeau Claque* –

Other nonsense, too, of course
oodles of white rabbits
and white panthers
that unfortunately devour
the rabbits just tricked into reality
there is really nothing to be done –

In any case it is snowing down
upon our bare heads
We are not cold
because we are only astral bodies

But in spite of that we can fly
and pass through walls

Breathlessly, arm in arm
we mount the spiral staircase of snow
in the mind of the dreamer
who is dreaming of us

faster and faster
because the steps are on fire
and the snow panthers are chasing us

They will devour us
There is really nothing to be done –

But we are very fast

The white talons
brush our hair
so ever softly

making us laugh

Apparition

When did she move in over there?

Her house disheveled by the wind
that long has only been inhabited by ghosts
rests on the other riverbank

Whenever I approach the window I look over –

I imagine names:
Aurora Ruth Penthesilea

Never do I see her clearly
always only her dancing silhouette
seconds at a time –

Sometimes the rocking chair upon her porch
is still swaying back and forth –

Today there is a book next to the stairs
its cover bent by the nightly dew
crimson like a butterfly upon a pin –

Or is it really an enormous butterfly sleeping there
like an open book?

Maybe she is blind
and is modeling a larger than life sized Apollo during the night?

Maybe she is farming golden frogs for the venomous arrows?

When she plays on the cembalo
the current swallows every sound –

I am certain that I saw her yesterday barefoot
sleepwalking on the rooftop –

Of course, she is my invention –

But even the river
that depending on the light is reminiscent
of the Mississippi or the Tiber
is only my invention
the window, too
and even this breathless moment
when her hand appears in the door open ajar
and pushes a little bowl of milk outside
for her invisible friend
the cougar

Moon, the Dark Side

The silence is sending me packages
day after day they grow larger –

Empty, of course –
It is all echoing space in there and shadows
into which I am bending
like into a cathedral –

Only once did a straw of light
fall out of the parcel –

Like some relic
of a bundle of light in which
who knows
what had been wrapped in –

Something very precious
very fragile
(but what?)
that someone else
(but who?)
in the same parcel of
stillness had sent –

This one blade of light
is stealing my sleep

I am constantly thinking about it

The Black Pencil

There it is –

Holy Nail
The shadow conductor's baton
Coffin for the next best mid-afternoon's sunbeam
Bottom of a Phaiakian galley dreaming its course –

Do not dare to speak to it!

Hermetica

The school at which I drop my daughter off
is a temple for giants –

I myself begin to shrink on its archaic steps
to the size of a bug that is leading a baby bug –

The lustrous hall
hears every whisper –

From afar litanies are resounding –
Nobody knows the divinity they are for –

Only later
when I return
when it is silent
when the afternoon sun is permeating
the empty hallways with incense

does it appear beyond the ecstatic windows
the large chestnut tree

and reveals its mysteries

The Great Mystery

Flaming more furiously than Zoroaster's light songs –

Deeper than the silence of Thomas Aquinas –

My daughter whispers into my ear
while I am dozing off
her hands a seashell pressing
her hair an electric aura
that is flaring up around me
while her breath
impinges
upon my eardrum
tiny
golden
pins

ALL EARS

GANZ OHR

All Ears

God – I am whispering my prayer
into your other ear –

Not into the enormous
stone Ear of Buddha
that is dripping down
as a weary infinite loop –

but in your tiny
trembling cicada ear
that must hear it all at once –

the shrieks during the massacre at the Ivory Coast
and in the same instance
the gentle mystical rustling
when Rafaela grooms her hair –

God – I know
that in reality you
only have a single ear
and that every prayer is far too large for it –

I kneel down
to listen
deep into your tiny cicada ear –

and my seething
tumultuous heartbeat

will be answered
by your unceasing hearing
presence

Voice

Look at me!

You will not be destroyed to dust like Semele!

I am not the dictator
with the thunderbolt hurling sunshades
whose name
not even rats dare to whisper –

There are no little bloodhounds circling my knees –

I am not asking you
what kind of fuming sacrifices
you offered up just now
in Venus' temple or Mithras' sanctuary –

I wander through the streets in the twilight
in the silken nightfall
while the meat axes are scrubbed
while clamoring children hurry after a ball
and pick up a scrunched
fig –

Come! Go with me! Now!

Eternity
passes so swiftly

Skyline with Lightning, 5 a.m.

None of those rumbling lustful summer storms –

This is an execution –

The gods have flicked on the electric chair
for Prometheus –

He is putting up a fight
shock after shock
blow after blow –

The air smells of singed hair –

Something is going terribly wrong –

Gasping desperately
he is still resisting –

The execution is called off –

for now

Ὁ υἱὸς τοῦ ἀνθρώπου

I
For the opening scene
Hollywood secured all rights
star spangled sky in the cinemascope
a Steven-Spielberg-comet

Kings close up with made-up faces
In the semidarkness a few
supernumeraries (shepherds) with flustered smiles

Everybody likes babies in the pictures!

The moronic ox
is fogging up the lens again
with his breath

II
Forty days in the desert
experiments with meditation and asceticism
that fail

No Buddhist enlightenment –

Only the wild goose chase of temptation

Satanas is filling the wasteland with noise
night and day
with his primitive rhythms
his basses madly cranked up

III
From now on
a prime candidate's schedule during elections
laying on of hands like autographs
miraculous healing without end
O save us from tax reform!
Remedy our hyperphagia and impotence!
Divine truth
in an interview en passé
Not a moment's reprieve
without a storm breaking loose somewhere
or a lynch mob needing appeasement –
He topples over the rummage tables
pours his spirit upon them and sparks
a hellfire
You brood of vipers!
And then he receives into his arms the blind infant
with a harelip

IV
Eyes wherever he goes
Eyes as those gathering around a burning temple
All of them eager to see the temple founder –

But who has ears?

The aging stripper
leaning against the club door –
The stockbroker
whose portfolios, all of them,
just imploded –
The Quaker's wife with her black hood
and incurable hiccup –

And, of course, the seven year old girl
holding her little brother by the hand –

Upon their master's request
they will head
straight for the arena
and offer up their lanky bodies
as lion's fodder
for the better entertainment of Nero

V
The end – shame for every Stoic!
Sweating blood panic ridden gasps

Whiplashing by the blind
who sees again

Beaten down by the lame
who walks again

Not even the roaches in the torture chamber
care much for his love

In his skull nothing but
pounding
pounding
pounding –

Two beams of wood
testify to the selective advantage
of nihilism

VI
Shovel brigades:
remove the cadaver!

Disinfect the streets
cleanse it from his hallowed brouhaha!

Flush his miserable divinity
down in the sewer!

VII
The light covered with slaked lime
the darkness sealed off

VIII
To be continued –

in another
universe

Beach Stroll

The great morning after –
the triumphant
all redeeming light –

Coke cans washed up on the shore
jellyfish condoms

and mixed in with that
bizarrely gleaming war time rubble
fanatically jagged sickle blades
of drowned Egyptians

and two steps onwards
a baby rattle

Biblical August Night

Comets shoot across the horizon
more than you can count –

Dull rhythms in the backyard
around the golden calf they are dancing
nude and bloodied –

In the meantime Judith
sets the table with jangling bracelets
for herself and Holofernes' head
on the adjacent balcony

How fondly she foretells and fulfills
his each and every wish before it's slurred
by his lips!

The bread knife is blinking in her left hand
while she taunts him with a bundle of grapes
using her right hand

We are resting lazily on the sofa:
Herod and Herodias

Some prophet is bellowing his admonishments
into the darkness drunk as a skunk

Down from the Tree of Knowledge
the glistening serpent is winding its way
through our apartment –

a bit dangerous as a pet

but so far it has only devoured minor demons –

oh yes! and yesterday one
of your sin-red shoes!

Gründerzeit Building

Pull down a shred of the cosmos blue
wallpaper with the birds of paradise on it –
this is just fan-fucking-tastic!

Termite infestation?
All of the walls are made of termites!
A single swarm of bumbling atoms!

Not to mention the hardwood floor!
At every step another purgatorial soul whines!

Better you don't take a look under the floor boards!

The line of previous tenants dates back to Gilgamesh –
battlefields full of corpses
lay beneath your feet, filled in with plaster

Not to mention
the manic hellfire
that is blazing through the boiler slit –

Metaphysical explosions
as though the Last Judgment were dawning!

None of the windows closes properly!
Nothingness is howling through the cracks –

But you can't leave –
there are no stairs and no stairwell
the Langobards have turned them to firewood –

So, drink your coffee in peace
and fetch a book from the never-ending
darkness of the library –

even if the lid buckles and curves
like space
and the pages are stained
by the gasping breath
of the dead

Nero's Serenade

Only the stones dare
to cringe inwardly –
We, the more sophisticated audience
have long since left our tortured bodies –
The infernal itchiness
the cascades of suppressed sneezing
the nausea, the bursting bladder
the sordidly stiff mask of enchantment –
far, far beneath us
while the soul is passing through higher pastures
of boredom –
As an absentee she is toddling amongst the stars
and, the pantheon stiffened up, she draws a beard
onto Jupiter who cannot resist
and cuts off the tip of Pluto's nose
And now she becomes fond of it
and starts slitting open the silence
slitting open its fish belly surreptitiously
and guts it lustfully –
Look at what is suddenly coming to daylight!
Weird entrails, hieroscopic somehow
only that there is no divination to be had
none at all –
except that the silence is endless
that it never never never ends
however deep you may cut
eternities of tripe eons of bowels –

Sounds crazy –
but there are moments
when I want my ears back
and my tortured body –
when my eyes are turned silver
from yearning and in want
of Nero's song

Night

In the end it is dust
saving the libraries –

Dust
whence we have emerged
whither we shall return

into which the finger draws
blazing signs

Dust
stirred up by breathing

Dance of the atoms
Dance of the planets

countless worlds

on every one of them a whispering serpent

on every one of them a crucified savior
rising from his grave

Joy of the resurrection
dancing dust angels

beneath the lamp

in the infinite silence
in the infinite night

of the library

Fortune Cookies & Firecrackers

Glückskekse & Knallbonbons

Fortune Cookies & Firecrackers

Ennui is a golden dragon. Feed him well!

* * *

He who builds a house of cards shouldn't be surprised when the moonlight moves in.

* * *

Leave the metaphysics to the salt shaker!

* * *

You've punched a tooth out of silence. How do you want to redeem that?

* * *

If somebody invites you to have a snowflake, oblige him and accept!

* * *

Lovers are nourished by fortune cookies – and don't even read their prophecies!

* * *

He who dines with cannibals should count his fingers after every course!

* * *

The avalanche will only embrace those whom it loves.

* * *

You still owe the light a favor.

***

Every triangle is lonesome and kisses its own elbow.

***

The fork's heartbeat keeps the universe warm.

***

Roaches are more arrogant than angels – and nearly as immortal.

***

With just a bit ambition you could sell firecrackers!

***

Only follow the Buddha when the rice grain agrees with him!

***

The shortest distance between two points is God.

***

Murders have been committed with toothpicks.

***

The wise man only sits down at the gambling table when he is certain he shall lose.

***

Listen to your umbrella! It is versed in the language of shadows.

Make sure you change the galaxy at the next opportunity!

***

He who orders an eagle for dinner is either a wise man or a braggart.

***

Stare into the cleavage of a demon, but never in its eyes!

***

Stars are sober creatures, but the paper napkins are dreamers.

***

Toss a brick into the next best window – and remember carefully where every single splinter landed!

***

This fly loves you! Prove that you're worthy!

***

The man of wisdom delves his finger into the candle flame and continues talking – in theory.

***

The chair over there is smiling like Buddha – please pick another seat!

***

Nothingness can be bribed with only a handful of snowflakes – at least for the time being.

***

Only frequent restaurants that reserve tables for ghosts!

* * *

Have the courage to whistle after the next best comet!

* * *

We accept all valid dreams.

* * *

Please exit this diner through the wall!

Passages in italics are in a foreign language in the original poem.

Natural Supernaturalism
On Ludwig Steinherr's Poetry

Paul-Henri Campbell

Natural Supernaturalism
On Ludwig Steinherr's Poetry

The Romantics have made skeptics of all of us. No wonder that particularly in Germany – where pathos was especially viral throughout the 19th century – poets of the last two generations or so sought a new approach to verse by eradicating the dainty effervescence of feeling from the ledgers of contemporary poetry. Sobering up from the strange intoxication of Romanticism, those modern poets have, however, left us in a climate of dispassionate objectivity in which perspicuity often goes hand in hand with sterility and reflective introspection is often tantamount to navel-gazing. In an atmosphere like this, Ludwig Steinherr seems out of place – and yet he may offer us a new understanding of what poetry could be.

While there is a tendency to transcribe verse from the pages of fashionable textbooks on aesthetics, Steinherr has embarked on a radical search for a fresh method, mood, and melody of that which is commonly referred to as the Art of Poetry. In the *Frankfurter Allgemeine Zeitung*, the literary scholar Wulf Segebrecht has ranked Steinherr among »the most powerful poets of today«.

I will now briefly offer a few remarks on his career and point out one aspect concerning his work. I, of course, do not claim that these remarks reflect little more than my (subjective) opinion as a translator and invite the reader to draw his or her own conclusions.

Born in 1962, Ludwig Steinherr came of age in a family with artistic roots in Munich, the capital of the Free State of Bavaria. His great-grandfather, Alois Roth, already had studied painting under Wilhelm von Lindenschmit at the local Academy of Visual Arts and practiced his craft in Munich throughout the decades before and around 1900. But young Ludwig did not seek a profession in the visual arts. Instead, he sought a dual citizenship in the *Land of Poets and Thinkers* by taking up philosophy at the University of Munich and by composing poetry. In 1985, he carried his first collection of poems off to the printers. Those first poems gathered under the title *Fluganweisung* (»Flight Instructions«) are filled with all the charm and awkwardness of a young man's enthusiasm, carefully calculated and measured by someone whose favorite high school subjects were Latin and Mathematics. Although in hindsight it seems amazing how these early attempts could have matured into the elegant and ductile verse of his manhood, one quickly realizes that it took a certain degree of confidence to find the flexible tone that so idiosyncratically marks his later work. Perhaps submitting his dissertation on G. W. F. Hegel and the analytical philosopher Willard »Van« Quine in 1995 eased his poetical approach. There are indeed a great many things that a philosophical mind could penetrate and explicate, but there are ever so many more things that only poetry can bring forth to language. In the early 1990s, there was suddenly an eruptive burst of poems, each book coming off the press lovelier than the one preceding it, at the time of *Vor der Erfindung des Paradieses* in 1993. Then awards and prizes began to accumulate, and in 2003 he was inducted into the Bavarian Academy of Fine Arts. He has since also been invited to literary conventions and festivals across Europe and has also given lectures in the United States. A selection of his work has been translated by Richard Dove and published in the United Kingdom.

With each new book his technique, his theme, his entire poetological outlook seemed fantastically altered. Only when one examines the enormous corpus of his work synoptically, when one examines it with relative distance and patience, one realizes the gradual infinitesimal steps towards that magnificent voice, which was to become the poetic idiom of the grown man. It is noteworthy that the event of the German Reunification and the end of the Cold War fell into those feverish years. And, even though Ludwig Steinherr's poetry isn't explicitly political, there is nevertheless – unmistakably - an inherent interest in negotiating the existential status quo. And what we may witness in these poems is the negotiation of a new cosmopolitan European psyche, a consciousness that presses onwards without looking away from its horrible past and without shying from its responsibility towards the cultural heritage of the Continent. Let us, for the time being, call this negotiation a *serene purpose*.

For instance, consider the poem »In the Bamberg Cathedral«. It was the last poem the Jewish literary critic Marcel Reich-Ranicki had singled out for review in his famous *Frankfurter Anthologie* before he passed away in September 2013. The poem must have struck a chord within the old editor, something he had wrestled with his entire life. The poem picks up a theme that was a shameful but common feature in ecclesiastical structures all across mediaeval Europe: the juxtaposition of Ecclesia and Synagoga which depicts, in the shape of two women, *Ecclesia* as a triumphant figure and the *Synagoga* as figure that is blindfolded to whatever had been thought to be »truth« in those Dark Ages. The juxtaposition was a common motif within the nocuous canon of mediaeval anti-Judaism. Without neglecting the atrocious nature of this female couple, however, Ludwig Steinherr engages the two figures in a meditation on the theory of history. A few lines into the poem, the narrative voice says: »This ought to turn into a poem / about pogroms and smoldering ovens –«. But it doesn't … and yet it does. The poem continues »But I am only able / to think about the musty varieté show / in which she the psychic could foretell«. Who is she, the psychic? Some lady on a back alley stage of Bamberg who professionally amuses tourists, or is the narrative voice still lingering with its initial impression within the ancient cathedral? The complex impression that makes this poem so unique is produced by its layering of multiple dimensions of perception: on an intellectual and mnemonic level we have the terrible history of the German war crimes, and on another level we have their ubiquity haunting every new experience; on an emotional and existential level we have minds going about their lives, reading »an unfinished love poem«, riding on the train »a return ticket to Munich« – but even the most naïve thought is thus haunted by the deflowered consciousness within which it exists.

There is indeed a constant lurid presence of the powers unseen in the work of Ludwig Steinherr. In »In the Bamberg Cathedral«, we are confronted with recent cultural history, but there are other magnitudes of consciousness floating around in his poetry as well. The piece »Garden in the Night When Nobody is Watching« sends the reader's imagination into a garden in which the bushes are reminiscent of erotic fantasy and the ants (strange enough) are symbols of powers operating beyond human perception: »the ants are searching for a signal / from the star that radio controls them«. Like some demiurge that is able to shift between parallel universes, the poet forces about collisions amongst various realities. In the closing lines of the poem mentioned just now, we read: »The hour at which Anubis God of the Dead / forces his jackal head through the fence / and wanders through his territory«. Anubis, of course, transports us into the timeless mythic reality of ancient Egypt, but this reality is merged with the more ordinary horticultural reality of a present day garden. In that garden during some forlorn hour of the night, a dog may be »forcing« its head through the »fence« when sounding out its »territory«. The lexical ambiguity employed here, as for instance with the word »territory« (German: »*Revier*«), initiates a controlled collision between the mythical anamnesis and the nocturnal perception. It thus modifies the image of »fence«, exposing its liminal nature. But the figure of Anubis is modified, too: we are reminded that – god or no god – he is a creature, belongs to the animal world of mythic imagination. This interpenetration of varying realms of reality, however, does not happen whimsically or, as other poets might say, »for artistic reasons«. In Ludwig Steinherr's cosmos, metaphor isn't some sort of pleasant decoration. By penetrating or piercing one reality with the order and logic of another reality, the semantic field of the poem is expanded. We partake in more than this or that reality. We are suddenly native to both dimensions while augmenting the imaginative potential of our own existential reality. A strange synthesis takes place while our consciousness is deflected, twisted, and sent into a new direction. Ludwig Steinherr does this often. Instances could easily be multiplied (e. g.: check out the optical illusions in »Shop Window with Antiquated Leica Cameras«).

I just said that his arrangements and collisions and mergers of reality do not occur without a purpose. This is not to say that they have an explicit intention. It doesn't even imply that we necessarily need to ascribe any meaning to this at all. If this division may be made at all, Ludwig Steinherr is an artist first and a thinker second. And yet there is an inescapable density of phenomena and imagery from realms of cultural history or myth. There is the frequency of the very maneuver described above. We may therefore suggest: here is a poet who believes there is something beyond our present empirical reality. There is a supernatural realm, not severed entirely from our empirical experience, but a realm that exerts its force upon the way we move in our everyday awareness, a realm that celebrates its intimate communion with our customary perception. Ludwig Steinherr leaves open the question of what that reality or those realities may be or mean. Instead, he produces verse for our delectation that holds a sort of added bonus in store for those who are willing to read into those surreal or mythical or fantastical layers – a sublime experience for those willing to immerse themselves into this habitual subtext of the supernatural.

And even though the supernatural imagery prevalent in his work comes from the banks of the Rhône and the slopes of the Monte Visio, even though Steinherr breathes with the Hebrews the scent of the almond tree and with the Greeks the lush air of the olive grove, even though his lines are littered with orgiastic parties, gunfights, Leica Cameras, investment banking, and Coke cans, the reader will never be put off by a phony notion of eclecticism. The reader will sense this serene purpose, forever inaudible. However many variables his work may include, the poet always seems to solve the equation and manages to hold together this vast assemblage under the great panoply of his verse.

Perhaps after reading into the complex layers of this rich substrata, the philosopher Vittorio Hösle (Notre Dame/USA) was persuaded to refer to Ludwig Steinherr as »a German metaphysical poet« who »like Paul Cézanne stares down into the dignity of each thing«. This is certainly one of the beautiful rewards that come from reading this poet: a feeling for the dignity of each thing, large or small; not life-altering, but radically changing our awareness for the deportment, movement, and melody of things.

Berlin, October 2013

Contents

The Secret Dominion

The Secret Dominion · 7
The Garden in the Night – when Nobody is Watching · 8
While Brewing Strong Coffee · 9

In the Darkness Your Third Shoulder Blade

Arrival, too Early · 13
In the Museum and Afterwards in the Rain · 14
Hallowed Twilight · 16
Side Chapel · 17
Naked · 18
Roman Nocturnal Stroll · 19
Looking at your Photo on the Plane · 20
Forensics · 22

The Museum of Beautiful Ideas

Shop Window with Antiquated Leica Cameras · 25
The Museum of Beautiful Ideas · 26
Blizzard in the Night · 28
Black Painter · 28
White Painter · 30
In the Bamberg Cathedral · 31
Giorgio de Chirico · 32
The Sensuous the Utmost Abstractness · 34
The Sculptor Says · 35

The Ghost Train with Living Ghosts

The Sudden Jolt of Autumn · 39
Localization · 40

Finale · 41
Library in Evening Light 1 · 42
Armageddon · 43
Cassiopeia Rests her Finger on her Lips · 44
The Ghost Train with Living Ghosts · 45
Gunfight at the OK Corral · 46
Library in Evening Light 2 · 48
Dark Autumn Afternoon – · 49
Maybe Gold · 50
Rain in the Night · 51
A Melody in Every Entity · 52
Night in November · 53
Untouchable · 54

ORANGES MOVING IN

Oranges Moving In · 59

SNOWY SPIRAL STAIRCASE

Afternoon Show · 65
House of the Spirit · 66
Chapeau Claque · 68
Apparition · 70
Moon, the Dark Side · 72
The Black Pencil · 73
Hermetica · 74
The Great Mystery · 75

ALL EARS

All Ears · 79
Voice · 80
Skyline with Lightning, 5 a.m.

Ὁ υἱὸς τοῦ ἀνθρώπου · 82
Beach Stroll· 86
Biblical August Night · 87
Gründerzeit Building · 88
Nero's Serenade · 90
Night · 91

FORTUNE COOKIES & FIRECRACKERS

Fortune Cookies & Firecrackers · 95

Ludwig Steinherr

BEFORE THE INVENTION OF PARADISE
Arc Publications, UK
Translated from the German by Richard Dove
Introduced by Jean Boase-Beier
Bilingual edition: German/English. Visible Poets series / edited by
Jean Boase-Beier.
ISBN 978-1904614-45-6, Paperback, £ 10,99
ISBN 978-1904614-94-4, Hardback, £ 13,99

Ludwig Steinherr is one of the most compelling new voices to have emerged in Germany since the late 1980s and this selection - the first to appear in English - from his 10 poetry collections published between 1985 and 2005 reflects the breadth and depth of his writing, ranging from its post-Celanian darkness to its insistence on light.

»Ludwig Steinherr's poetry, both profound and accessible, seems an obvious candidate for English translation. For one thing, it gives us a picture of the things that concern many modern German poets: its themes are silence, memory, knowing and the impossibility of knowing, the everyday and what is beyond. It also shares with much contemporary German poetry its spareness of style, lack of ornamentation and even of punctuation. Afterlife is as important as backstory. And so textual gaps, that play so important and poignant a role in modern German poetry, are here not just silent monuments for loss, but they are also the place for the reader to enter into«.
Jean Boase-Beier

www.arcpublications.co.uk

Richard Dove

Aus einem früheren Leben
From a Previous Life
Poetry
English/German
Lyrikedition 2000 (2003)
ISBN 978-3-86250-032-7, Paperback, € 19.90

»From a Previous Life« brings »departed days« back to the present. In his collection of English poems, Richard Dove offers us work that has principally been composed between 1976 and 1986. Thematically, he is concerned with the societal shifts on the British Isles of that period, as well as with (mainly) classical and German literary models. But Paris and the infamous Marquis de Sade are also featured in the lavish spectrum presented by this cosmopolitan poet, who navigates dexterously within various literary forms. The German translations have been prepared by various prominent poets. In doing so, they offer insights into the plurality of voices and modes of expression prevalent in contemporary German verse.

Since his relocation to Munich in 1987, Richard Dove has predominantly written in German. In 2002, he published a volume of poems entitled »Farbfleck auf einem Mondrian-Bild« (»Color Stain on a Mondrian Painting«), which the German poet and critic Durs Grünbein warmly welcomed as an »exciting little book«.

www.lyrikedition-2000.de

PAUL-HENRI CAMPBELL

SPACE RACE
Poetry
English/German
fhl-Verlag (2012)
ISBN 3-94282-921-5, € 14.00

»Space Race« retraces space exploration in lyrical verse. Paul-Henri Campbell has taken historic moments, such as the Sputnik Shock, the death of Yuri Gagarin, the Apollo Space Program, or the Challenger disaster, and has transformed these milestones into elements of a great modern day mythology. In doing so, he has fused technology with literature, history with myth, and religion with the heavens in ways that are as bizarre as they are enchanting.

AM ENDE DER ZEILEN
AT THE END OF DAYS
Poetry
English/German
fhl-Verlag (2013)
ISBN 9-42829-568, € 14.00

»At the End of Days« is a collection of poems on epochal change. The maiden flight of the Concorde, the aircraft carrier USS Kitty Hawk, the city of Detroit, a pacemaker. These things and places are ingredients in Paul-Henri Campbell's poetry. His work is postmodern hagiography, a *Legenda aurea* on the threshold from the mechanical age to the digital era. Transported into a new reality, supersonic airplanes, battleships, or decayed landscapes suddenly develop the power to be more than mere mechanics, so that the fate of an entire period may be deciphered by re-reading it along the lines of the objects that made history.

www.fhl-verlag.de